CAMBRIDGE PRIMARY
Mathematics
Starter Activity Book

C

Name: _____

Cherri Moseley and Janet Rees

CAMBRIDGE
UNIVERSITY PRESS

University Printing House, Cambridge CB2 8BS, United Kingdom

Cambridge University Press is part of the University of Cambridge.

It furthers the University's mission by disseminating knowledge in the pursuit of education, learning and research at the highest international levels of excellence.

Information on this title: education.cambridge.org

First published 2016

Printed in Dubai by Oriental Press

A catalogue record for this publication is available from the British Library

ISBN 978-1-316-50912-8 Paperback

This book is part of the Cambridge Primary Maths project. This is an innovative combination of curriculum and resources designed to support teachers and learners to succeed in primary mathematics through best-practice international maths teaching and a problem-solving approach. To get involved, visit **www.cie.org.uk/cambridgeprimarymaths**.

Introduction

This set of three mathematics Starter Activity Books (A–C) will help to develop children's skills and knowledge to be ready for entry to primary school.

The activities are written to help parents/carers and pre-school teachers to support children in the Early Years. They are also ideal for Grade 1 teachers to ensure children are ready and equipped with the skills they need at the start of the Primary Curriculum.

These books are written to encourage learning through play, and in such a clear and accessible way that they can be used by parents/carers to support their child's learning and development at home.

To complete this series, there is an accompanying set of 12 activity books for Primary Mathematics Grades 1–6. There is a Skills Builder and a Challenge activity book for each of the six Curriculum Framework stages to support and broaden the depth of mathematics learning.

How to use the books

The three books are written in a three-term approach (A, B and C). They can be used as standalone or as a supplementary to the Cambridge Primary Mathematics core scheme for Grade 1.

The coverage of learning objectives provides the basis of an Early Years framework to allow pre-schoolers to reach a confident level of mathematics to transition to primary Grade 1. Activities are written to underpin Cambridge International Examinations Primary Mathematics Curriculum Framework Stage 1—see the outline of coverage on the next page.

The varied set of activities support different learning styles: working individually, in pairs, in groups, at kindergarten/pre-school or at home, and ideas for greater challenge are provided for children who are more confident.

Each activity follows a consistent approach:

- an instructional 'what to do/how to play the game' guides the teacher or parent/carer through each activity, providing advice on how to approach the content, and ideas of how to give extra support or to extend children's learning
- a vocabulary list for guided reading, to encourage the learning of key mathematical terms

- a list of required resources in 'You will need'—resources are kept simple and accessible for use at home
- space to record results in the book as well as freedom to revisit the activity later
- link to the key area of focus is given in the footnote on each page.

Note: when a 'spinner' is given in an activity, put a paper clip flat on the page so the end is over the centre of the spinner. Place the pencil point in the centre of the spinner, through the paperclip. Hold the pencil firmly and spin the paperclip to generate a result.

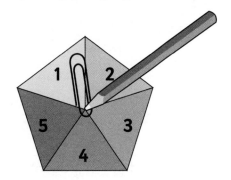

How to track progress

End-of-term assessments are given at the end of each book. Each activity is supported by an explanation of how to support the child and what the activity is testing.

Numeral practice is encouraged in each book, and formalised by a fill-in chart at the back. The intention is that children practise a particular number as and when it would be helpful for them. It would not be helpful to ask children to complete a whole page at one time.

A comment box is provided at the end of each book to write short notes about the children's successes and, if appropriate, about anything they need further help with.

Comments

Contents

For the teacher or parent/carer: the list below shows the content of this book, and how the activities underpin the Cambridge International Examinations Primary Mathematics Curriculum Framework Stage 1.

Buttons

Draw the matching number of buttons on each coat.

The first one is done for you.

What to do

Count along the number track to 7 together.

Help the children to draw the correct number of buttons on each coat to match the number written on the pocket.

Count the buttons together, with the children, to check.

0	1	2	3	4	5	6	7

Staircase

Complete the staircase numbers.

What to do

The children should be able to count to 7 confidently.

The staircase shows the 'quantity value' of each number.

The children can count along the boxes at the bottom, or they can count the blocks in each tower to find the totals. They write the appropriate number in each box.

Children draw that number of objects in each tower, one in each block.

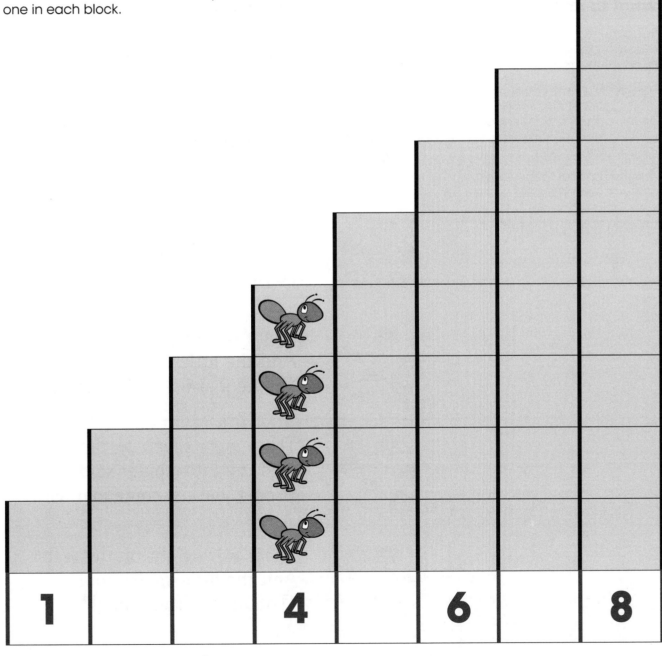

| 1 | | | 4 | | 6 | | 8 |

Spiders

Vocabulary

0, 1, 2, 3, 4, 5, 6, 7, 8,

more than,

less than,

how many?

What to do

Read the rhyme to the children, pausing regularly to count the spiders.

Talk about how there is one more spider in each verse on this page and one fewer (less) spider in each verse on the facing page.

This rhyme is set to the tune of *There were 10 in the bed*. You could teach the children to sing along with it.

There was one on the web
And the little spider said,
"Come join me, come join me!"

There were two on the web
And the little spider said,
"Come join us, come join us!"

There were three on the web
And the little spider said,
"Come join us, come join us!"

There were four on the web
And the little spider said,
"Come join us, come join us!"

There were five on the web
And the little spider said,
"Come join us, come join us!"

There were six on the web
And the little spider said,
"Come join us, come join us!"

There were seven on the web
And the little spider said,
"Come join us, come join us!"

There were eight on the web
And the little spider said,
"Too many! Too many!"

So they all ran about and one fell off,
There were seven on the web
And the little spider said,
"Too many! Too many!"

So they all ran about and one fell off,
There were six on the web
And the little spider said,
"Too many! Too many!"

So they all ran about and one fell off,
There were five on the web
And the little spider said,
"Too many! Too many!"

So they all ran about and one fell off,
There were four on the web
And the little spider said,
"Too many! Too many!"

So they all ran about and one fell off,
There were three on the web
And the little spider said,
"Too many! Too many!"

So they all ran about and one fell off,
There were two on the web
And the little spider said,
"Too many! Too many!"

So they all ran about and one fell off,
There was one on the web
And the little spider said,
"Just me, Hooray!"

0	1	2	3	4	5	6	7	8

How many spiders?

Count the spiders on each web.

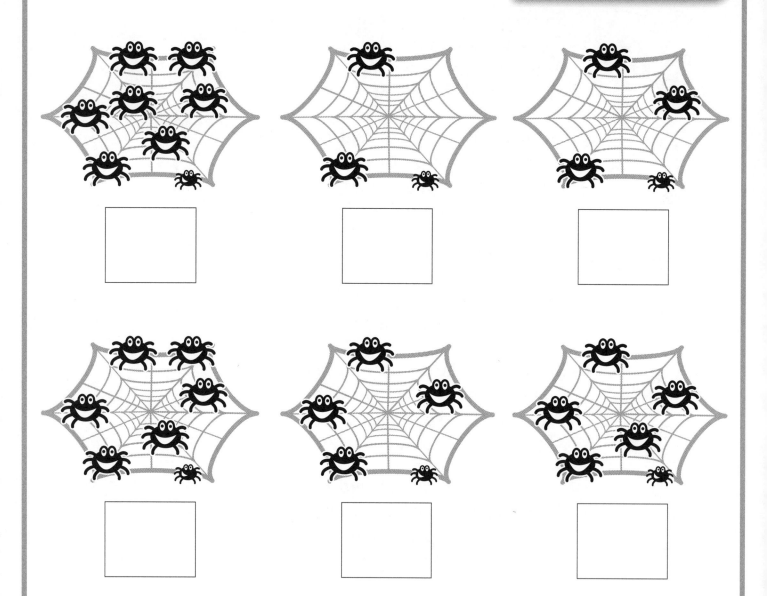

What to do

Talk about which web has more or fewer (less) spiders than a particular web.

Help the children to count the spiders on each web and to write the matching number in the box.

0	1	2	3	4	5	6	7	8

Spin for the spiders' legs!

Draw the spiders' legs.

You will need: a pencil and a paperclip to use the spinner

How to play the game

This is a game for one or two children.

The children spin the spinner to find out how many legs to draw on a spider.

By the end of the game, each spider must have 8 legs.

For a two-player game, the children either claim four spiders each or the player who draws the eighth leg on any particular spider can colour in the box under that spider.

The winner is the player with more spiders in their own colour.

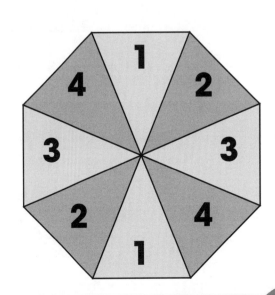

Bone collector

Collect the bones.

Counting up to 10 and back

How to play the game

This is a game for two children.

The children take turns to roll the dice. Based on the score, they move from the kennel, along their own path to the dustbin to collect a bone.

When they have collected a bone, they take it back along the path to their kennel, using the dice to determine the number of steps, as before. Then they move back to the dustbin for another bone.

When all the bones have been claimed, children count how many each of them has.

The winner is the player with more bones.

You will need: a counter for each player, a 1–6 dice, 15 yellow counters for bones

Bubbles

Join each statement to the correct number.

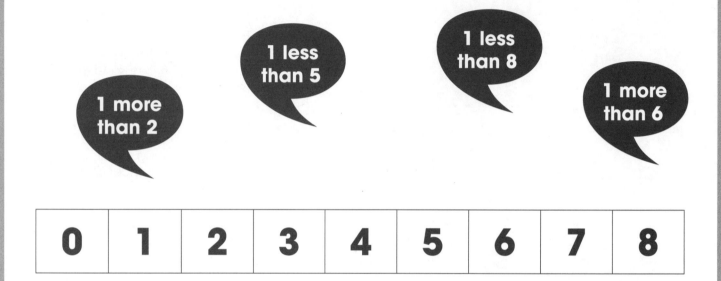

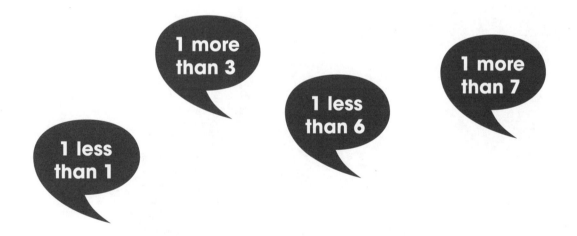

What to do

Revise 'one more and one less' with the children, using everyday objects and the number track.

Then the children draw a line to join each bubble to the correct number. Some children may need help with reading the instructions.

Grids

Complete the grids.

Vocabulary

0, 1, 2, 3, 4, 5, 6, 7, 8, 9, 1 more than, 1 less than, how many?

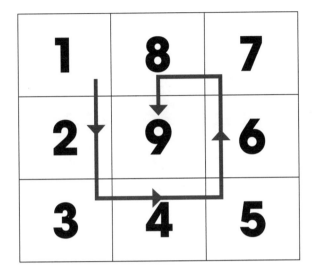

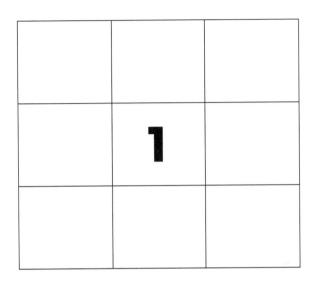

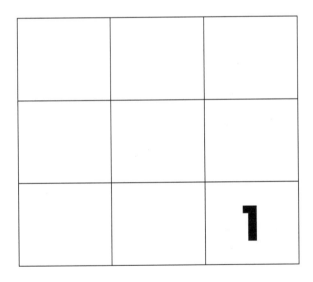

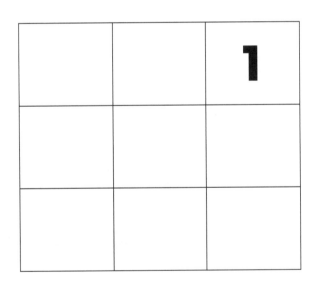

What to do

The first grid contains the numbers 1 to 9 with a continuous line joining the numbers in order.

Help the children to complete the other grids, placing the numbers 2 to 9 in any order they choose. Then they must draw a line joining the numbers, in order. Each line may cross itself at some point.

The number 1 has been written in each grid to make sure children start their numbering in different places.

0	1	2	3	4	5	6	7	8	9

Growing grids

Complete the grid.

Vocabulary

0, 1, 2, 3, 4, 5, 6, 7, 8, 9, 10,
1 more than, 1 less than,
how many?

What to do

The children count the animals in each row, from 1 to 8, and write in the missing numbers.

For rows 9 and 10, they draw the correct number of animals, copying the picture that is provided.

Fishy numbers

How many? Write the numbers.

Vocabulary

0, 1, 2, 3, 4, 5, 6, 7, 8, 9, 10,
1 more than, 1 less than,
how many?

What to do

The children count how many there are of each different animal or object.
Some children will find it helpful to cross out each object as they count it.

They record the totals in the correct boxes.

Domino addition

Complete each addition.

Vocabulary

0, 1, 2, 3, 4, 5, 6, 7, 8, 9, 10, more than, less than, add, addition, equals, how many?

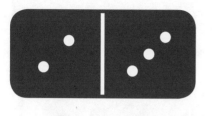

2 + 3 = 5

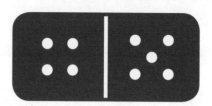

___ + ___ = ___

___ + ___ = ___

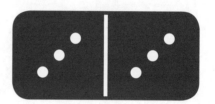

___ + ___ = ___

___ + ___ = ___

___ + ___ = ___

What to do

The children count the spots on each part of the domino. Then they work out how many spots there are altogether on the whole domino. Some children will count all the spots, others may be able to count on.

For further practice, children can add the spots on a set of real dominos, but remove from the set any that have totals greater than 10.

0	1	2	3	4	5	6	7	8	9	10

Jumping back

Where will each creature land?

Vocabulary

0, 1, 2, 3, 4, 5, 6, 7, 8, 9, 10, more than, less than, add, addition, equals, how many?

Jump back 2. Colour the square where the frog lands.

0	1	2	3	4	5	6	7	8	9	10

Jump back 5. Colour the square where the kangaroo lands

0	1	2	3	4	5	6	7	8	9	10

Jump back 4. Colour the square where the rabbit lands.

0	1	2	3	4	5	6	7	8	9	10

Jump back 6. Colour the square where the flea lands.

0	1	2	3	4	5	6	7	8	9	10

What to do

Act out the activity on a floor number track before asking the children to complete the tracks above.

Discuss counting back with the children as they investigate jumping back on the number track.

Ten pink flowers

Ten pink flowers, growing when it's fine,
A slug came and ate one, then there were nine.

Nine pink flowers, growing through the gate,
Thomas came and picked one and then there were eight.

Eight pink flowers, beginning to redden,
A bird came and pecked one and then there were seven.

Seven pink flowers, propped up by sticks,
A mole came wriggling and then there were six.

Six pink flowers, glad to be alive,
A ball came and squashed one and then there were five.

What to do

Read the rhyme to the children.

Use the illustrations to talk about 'one more' and 'one less'.

Then the children can complete the number track and use
it to practise counting back from 10.

Five pink flowers, not any more,
A mouse came and nibbled one and then there were four.

Four pink flowers, as bright as can be,
A ladybird came munching and then there were three.

Three pink flowers, none of them were new,
A caterpillar came crawling, and then there were two.

Two pink flowers, happy in the sun,
Dad came collecting and then there was one.

One pink flower, the only one I've got,
I'll keep it on my windowsill, now planted in a pot.

0		2	3		5	6		8		10

Jungle sizes

Draw an animal that is shorter than the giraffe.

Draw a monkey higher up the tree.

Draw a smaller elephant.

What to do

There is no expectation that children will know the relative sizes of real animals for this activity.

The creatures in their pictures need to be shorter, higher or smaller than the creatures as drawn on the page.

Snakes

Colour the longest snake red.

Colour the shortest snake blue.

Colour the thin snake green.

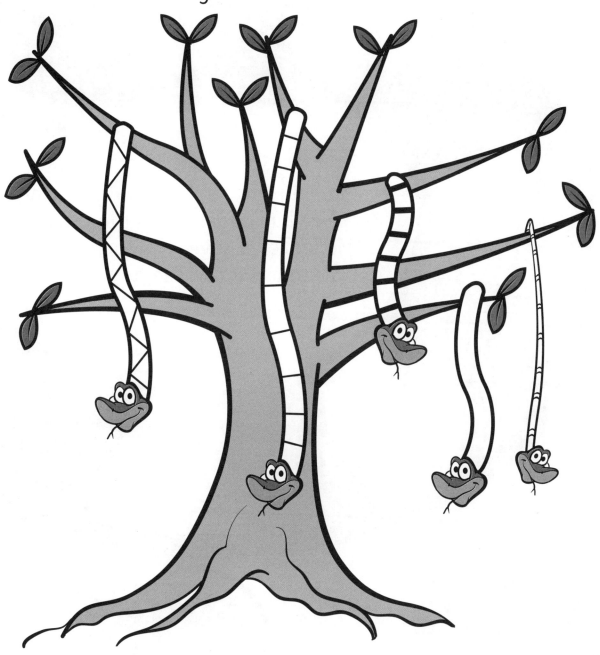

What to do

Help the children to follow the instructions. Make sure that they recognise which snake is longest, which is shortest.

If necessary, shade over the instructions lightly with the appropriate colours.

Who will win the race?

Start

Sammy the snail is slowly moving
See him slide across the grass,
He leaves a silver trail behind him
So that we can see he's passed.

0
5
1
4
2
3

How to play the game

This is a game for two players. The children choose to be either the horse or the snail. They take turns to spin the spinner and move that number of places.

0 means 'Stay where you are for that turn.'

The first player to reach 'Finish' is the winner.

Discuss how the winner must have travelled faster.

Galloping, galloping
How fast my horse can go,
It's only when he's tired
He goes slow, slow, slow.

Finish

Hungry frog

Complete the table.

Vocabulary

0, 1, 2, 3, 4, 5, 6, 7, 8, 9, 10, more than, fewer than, table, how many?

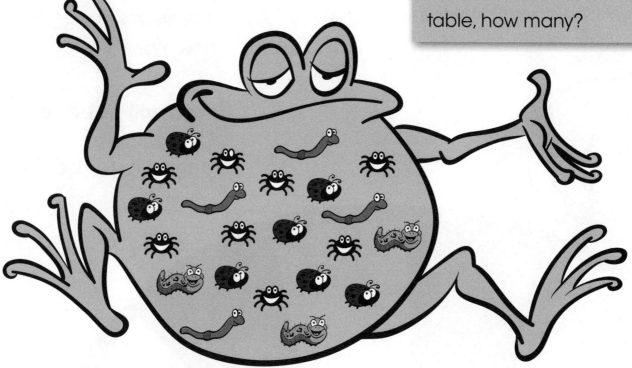

Animal	How many?
(caterpillar)	
(ladybird)	
(worm)	
(spider)	

What to do

The children count how many there are of each animal in the frog's stomach.

Then they write the number in the correct row of the table.

They use the information to complete the two sentences. They can write or draw to fill the gaps.

Frog ate more _____ than _____.

Frog ate fewer _____ than _____.

Sorting animals

Where does each animal belong?

4 legs	not 4 legs

There are more animals with _____ than _____.

(4 legs, not 4 legs)   (4 legs, not 4 legs)

What to do

The children sort the animals into the correct boxes .

They could either draw the animals or draw a line from each animal to the correct box.

Children choose the correct words to complete the sentence.

Animal spinner

What to do

The children spin the spinner to find out which animal square to tick or colour.

They use the number track to keep count of the number of spins.

After 10 spins, children use the information in the block graph to answer the questions.

You will need: a pencil and a paperclip to use the spinner

How many ? _____

How many ? _____

How many ? _____

How many ? _____

How many ? _____

How many  ? _____

| 0 | 0 | 1 | 2 | 3 | 4 | 5 | 6 | 7 | 8 | 9 | 10 |

How many?

Count the vehicles and write the number below.

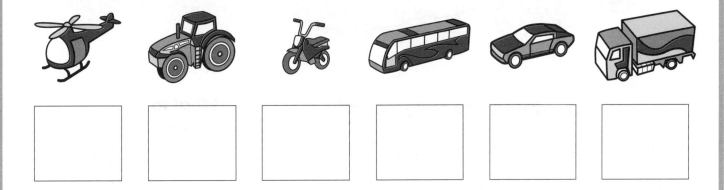

What to do

This activity will give the children opportunities to demonstrate their counting and recording skills within 10.

Compare the animals

Draw a ring around the taller giraffe.

Draw a ring around the shortest snake.

Draw a ring around the higher bird.

Draw a ring around the longest crocodile.

Draw a ring around the smallest animal.

What to do

This activity gives children the opportunity to demonstrate some understanding of the language of comparative measures.

Explain the instructions, supporting reading as needed.

Numeral practice

1									1
2	2	2	'						2
3	3	?	'						3
4	4	4	'						4
5	5	5	'						5

What to do

Encourage children to practise writing numerals in wet and dry sand, then writing them in the grid or with foam, paint, chalk and chunky pens, and/or modelling them in dough and in many other ways.

This page and the following page give children the opportunity to practise numeral formation.

Children should practise a particular number as and when it would be helpful. It would not be helpful to ask children to complete a whole page at one time.

Numeral practice

6	6	6	‚					6
7	7	7						7
8	8	8	‚					8
9	9	9	‚					9
10	10	10	10					10

Comments